Written by: Ilana Danneman
Illustrated by Debra Sifen

ISBN #978-0-9860749-6-7
10 9 8 7 6 5 4 3 2 1

"If I am not for me, who is for me; and if I am (only) for myself, what am I? And if not now, when?"
— Hillel, Ethics of the Fathers, 1:14

When I was a young girl, my mother handed me a letter that had been dictated by my grandfather, Isidore Sirota (aka Joe the Jew) and typed by my Aunt Claire Renov, his oldest daughter, a few weeks before he died. In that letter he explained his journey to Atlanta, how much he loved his family and how he had come to love the community he had befriended as a grocer in the 1930s-1950s. My grandfather's story is not so unique as many Jewish families owned grocery stores during those times and became a part of the city culture and local people. Typically a family, such as mine, would live on top or behind the store.

But my grandfather stood out, not only in his ability as a grocer, but by his character. He was a man of the people who aided those in need. I did not have the privilege of knowing my grandfather but I was named in his memory and he left me a peek into his life. For that, I am extremely grateful and to my mother for preserving the letter. I have also had the privilege of interviewing my mother, Isabelle Sirota Maslia and my father Albert M. Maslia, as to what it was like growing up in Atlanta in the 30's and 40's. Their stories have been recorded at Story Corps at the Atlanta History Center.

But this is not just my story, this is a story that belongs to all of us and I was beyond delighted when Debra Sifen, an accomplished illustrator (Manny's a Thief, We Want Life, Then I Got 3 Scoops, Hair of the Dog Comic, Seaweed's Oasis), and devoted friend agreed to illustrate Joe's Market. She too was raised in Atlanta. Debra and I both hope this story will not only touch your interests but your hearts and souls. We all can relate to Joe the Jew, as he so fondly became known. Many may earn a living differently than Joe, but how we treat others and how we deal with each situation, can define our character and the legacies we leave behind.

With much love and blessings,

Ilana

To Mom

Joe's Market is a story of a Jewish grocer
in the 1930's, and how he affected his community.

Based on an original letter
written by Isidore Sirota (Joe, the Grocer)
in 1962, the story is told through the eyes of
his daughter, who is now a grandmother herself.
This is a story of Mr. Sirota's journey to Atlanta,
the opening of his store, moving his family,
and learning to love his customers.

Bubby, tell me a story!

I will tell you a story while you fill the bag with onions for the chicken soup I am making tonight. What kind of story do you want to hear?

Tell me a story about when you were little and you would go to the grocery store!

Well I was born in the Bronx, which is a borough of New York City. But when I was 3 years old my father moved our family to Atlanta to open our own grocery store!

Now please go get me 5 potatos - BIG ONES! You never know if someone else might stop by and want some of my delicious soup!

My parents started out quite poor. They barely had enough money to pay the milkman, and the baker would give them a loaf of bread on credit.

When my father had only ONE DIME left he used that dime to go look for work.

My father borrowed money from the bank.
He used some of the money to buy food
for my mother, my two older sisters and me.
With the rest of the money he bought a
bus ticket to Atlanta. He had a friend
in Atlanta who was going to help him find work.

My father had to change buses 4 times
before he arrived. It was a long trip,

All we need now is some carrots and celery and we'll be ready to get this soup cooking!

My father's friend helped him find a vacant store on the corner of Fraser and Fulton Street.

With the help of friends and the money left from the bank loan...

FRASER

FULTON

JOE'S MARK

APPLES

My father bought a refrigerator and a meat counter. With the rest of the money he bought stock and supplies. My father said it was the BEST grocery store in the ENTIRE WORLD! He called it "JOE'S MARKET".

And my father wouldn't have traded it for ANYTHING, even GIMBAL's fancy department store in New York City!

My parents owned the grocery store and worked in it. We lived behind the store and on top of it. There was a small window separating our house from the store. I would cry for my mother as I couldn't go in the store while they were working...

...Now we need a fresh chicken for the soup.
You know when I was little we had to pluck the feathers and clean the chicken ourselves!

Joe was my father's middle name. His first name was Isidore, but my father thought "Joe" would be a better fit with the local names. However, at the corner there was a hotdog stand operated by a man who was ALSO named Joe. To tell them apart, the people in the neighborhood started to call my father, "Joe the Jew".

He considered this an honorable distinction!

As time passed, the store felt more like home and Joe became part of the community.

Joe liked to help people.

He helped collect $50 bail for a customer who had been put in jail. The man was so grateful he paid my father back EVERY PENNY!

Once, another customer was going to lose all of his furniture because he couldn't pay the rent.
Joe was happy to help. Joe pleaded with the policeman not to take his friend's furniture. Joe made a deal...

The policeman agreed to leave the furniture if Joe would donate $5 to the policeman's wife's favorite charity. Joe said it was the best bargain.
Just one man helping another!

People came to trust Joe and his market. If other stores sold watermelons for 25 cents, Joe would sell his for 10 cents. 10 CENTS!!! And Joe would pick out the BEST watermelons for each customer. If they didn't like the one they bought they could bring it back and Joe would give them another one at NO COST!
On a busy, hot summer day, Joe could sell 200 watermelons, making 2 cents on each one. That's 4 dollars!

Well, that was a lot of money back then.

Joe was a good businessman.

Joe worked hard.

Every day he would take a pushcart and hire a young boy to take him to the large produce market. There he would fill up his cart and push it all the way back to his store.

People in the neighborhood would be visiting friends and they would often ask them,

"Where did you get this delicious meat?"

AT JOE'S MARKET, OF COURSE!

WELL, I'M GOING TO BUY MY MEAT THERE FROM NOW ON TOO!

Even the other grocery store owners and business owners came to love Joe's Market.

Sometimes the market was packed full of people!

The other store owners would say, "Thanks to Mr. Joe our neighborhood is a busy place!"

Eventually, Joe sold his market.
The city tore it down and built a
Stadium Hotel in its place.

But if I close my eyes,
I can still see my father's market.
I can see the door, the produce,
the meat counter.
I can see the cans of kerosene.
I can see my mother and sisters
working in the store.
I can see people shopping.

And I can see Joe the Jew!

Chicken Soup Recipe

Ingredients:

- 1 cut up onion
- 4-5 stalks of celery cut up
- 4-5 peeled and chopped carrots
- 1 large, peeled cut up potato
- 1 cut up chicken
- 1 tablespoon of salt
- seasonings of your choice
- love

Directions:
Place all ingredients in large crockpot. Fill the crockpot with water. Cook 6-8 hours on low heat. You can also cook on the stove. Bring to a boil and let it simmer for 45 minutes.

Enjoy and freeze left overs to use when someone needs chicken soup!

Isidore Joel Sirota was born December 27, 1895
in Russia and immigrated to Argentina
and then to the United States in 1921.
He started his new life in New York City and
eventually moved to Atlanta, Georgia in 1935.

His market was loved by all who came
to purchase foods and goods, and
he was known by those who loved him as
"Joe the Jew".

Left top: Isidore Sirota, Isabelle Sirota Maslia, Alisa Maslia (Austin),
Albert Maslia, Rose Levitas Sirota. Bottom left: Morris Maslia, Sheryl
Maslia (Rechtman). Photo taken 1959.

About the author (pictured with her mother Isabelle Maslia):
Ilana Danneman lives in Atlanta, GA and works as a pediatric physical therapist, blogger, product developer, product videographer and catalog director for children with special needs. Her love is creating something new, spending time with people, hiking, writing and snuggling with her dog. She also likes to find the light in the dark, God in each moment and having deep meaningful conversations. She is the author of A Tale of Two Souls (2014) and the blog Married To a Yid. She can be reached at kitov18@gmail.com

About the artist: The granddaughter of immigrants and an immigrant herself to Canada, Debra Sifen can appreciate the journey of Isidore Joe Sirota. Amidst her scattered career of illustrator and cartoonist, mother, daughter, teacher and wife, Debra has illustrated several children's books including Who Wants Life?, Manny's a Thief!, Then I Got 3 Scoops, as well as Ilana's last book Tale of Two Souls. Working from her studio in Toronto, with the help and inspiration of her dog, Sammy, and her husband, Reid, Debra also works on two comic strips, Seaweed's Oasis and Hair of the Dog. You can enjoy more of her work at www.seaweedsoasis.com and HairoftheDogComics on Facebook.

www.ingramcontent.com/pod-product-compliance
Lightning Source LLC
Chambersburg PA
CBHW040024050426
42452CB00002B/119